School-Age Care Environment Rating Scale

Thelma Harms
Frank Porter Graham Child Development Center
University of North Carolina at Chapel Hill
Chapel Hill, North Carolina

Ellen Vineberg Jacobs
Department of Education
Concordia University
Montreal, Quebec

Donna Romano White
Center for Research in Human Development
Concordia University
Montreal, Quebec

TEACHERS COLLEGE PRESS

Teachers College
Columbia University
New York and London

Published by Teachers College Press,
1234 Amsterdam Avenue, New York, NY 10027

Manufactured in the United States of America

ISBN 0–8077–3507–8

09   08   07   06   10   9   8

Contents

Acknowledgments

The *School-Age Care Environment Rating Scale* (SACERS) is a joint United States–Canadian effort which has benefited from the many close professional relationships established among early childhood researchers and practitioners from both countries. The SACERS is the newest scale in the series of program assessment instruments that originated with the Early Childhood Environment Rating Scale (ECERS) (Harms & Clifford, 1980). The three previous scales provided the model for developing the SACERS. We want to acknowledge the importance to this project of work done by Richard M. Clifford and Debby Cryer on the three other scales in the ECERS series.

In the five years that we have been working on the SACERS, many colleagues on both sides of the border have been extremely helpful. Louise Chartrand piloted the earliest version of the SACERS in Montreal, Quebec. Kay Albrecht, Carollee Howes, Eddie Locklear, Nancy Marshall, and Barbara Vandenbergh from the United States and Pat Golian, Nory Siberry, Madeleine Baillargeon, and Wilma Van Staaldumen from Canada served as experts in the content validity study. The reliability and validity studies conducted in Montreal, Quebec City, and Toronto involved Carole Bouchard, Jennifer Grant, Renée Roberts, Sandy Gabriel, Vali Fugulin, and Hélène Larouche as raters.

We are grateful for the encouragement and cooperation given to the project by Judith Levkoe, Nory Siberry and the staff of the school-age care programs conducted by the YMCA of Greater Toronto. Thanks also to Barbara Vandenbergh and her colleagues from the North Carolina Cooperative Extension Service who field-tested the scale in programs served by their agency.

We want to thank the Commission des Écoles Catholiques de Montréal and the individual schools in Montreal and Quebec City that participated in our studies.

The Special Needs Supplementary Items were originally developed by Don Bailey, Richard M. Clifford, and Thelma Harms of the Frank Porter Graham Child Development Center, and were revised by Thelma Harms and Debby Cryer.

We especially want to recognize our colleagues Debby Cryer of the University of North Carolina at Chapel Hill and Madeleine Baillargeon of Université Laval for serving as critical reviewers of the scale throughout its development.

The impressive computer skills and extraordinary patience of Cathy Riley were responsible for the usable design of the scale. The artwork for the cover was done by Denise Burgess, cover layout by Gina Harrison.

The Canadian reliability studies were completed under a grant from Health and Welfare Canada, Child Care Initiatives Fund.

Finally, we want to thank the many teachers and children in whose programs we observed and tried out the various versions of the scale. Their patience and openness made the development and field-testing of the SACERS a pleasant experience.

T. Harms
E. Jacobs
D. White
1995

Development of the SACERS

RATIONALE

School-age child care is nonparental care that is provided for children of elementary school age. The need for school-age child care has existed for as long as single working parents and dual career families have had children in elementary school, because the hours of operation of most elementary schools do not correspond to the standard business day. Families also need care for their school-age children while the parent is taking courses or when the family is in a crisis situation. In the United States in 1991, approximately 1.7 million school-age children were enrolled in 49,500 formal before and/or after school programs (Seppanen, deVries, & Seligson, 1993). Canadian statistics indicate that 67% of families with children 6-9 years of age must make arrangements for either full- or part-time child care due to their work schedule (Lero, Goelman, Pence, Brockman, & Nuttall, 1992).

In both the United States and Canada, elementary schools, community and recreation centers, preschool child care centers, and family child care homes have responded to this obvious need for supervision during out-of-school hours by developing school-age care programs. Both the facilities and the program content differ from one program to another. Some programs focus on recreational activities so that the children can have the same extracurricular opportunities that are available to children who return home at the end of the school day. Others focus on enhancing children's learning by offering a more academically oriented program. In yet other programs, there is an emphasis on the creative arts including the visual arts, music, and drama. One must also consider that school-age child care programs enroll children from 5 to 12 years of age. Given this broad age range, it is essential to offer activities that meet the widely differing needs and interests of children over a 7-year age span.

In order to develop a comprehensive rating scale for school-age child care programs, the authors drew from a number of sources. Rather than proposing a particular program philosophy, the SACERS is based on criteria for developmental appropriateness for school-age children. Definitions of quality, such as the *Quality Criteria for School-Age Child Care Programs* (Albrecht, 1991), and extant instruments, such as *Assessing School-Age Child Care Quality* (ASQ) (O'Connor, 1991) and the *Assessment Profile for Early Childhood Programs* (Abbott-Shim & Sibley, 1987), were reviewed. Decisions regarding quality indicators were also based on research, including Canadian studies (Baillargeon, Betsalel-Presser, Joncas, & Larouche, 1993; Betsalel-Presser & Joncas, 1994; Jacobs, White, Baillargeon, & Betsalel-Presser, 1991; White, 1990) and studies conducted in the United States (Galambos & Garbarino, 1983; Vandell & Corasaniti, 1988; Vandell, Henderson, & Wilson, 1988). Best practice as presented in the literature (Seligson & Allenson,

1993) was also taken into consideration so that the scale would reflect current ideas of what should be done to meet the developmental needs of school-age children.

Most important, the SACERS is an adaptation of the *Early Childhood Environment Rating Scale* (ECERS) (Harms & Clifford, 1980). The SACERS is similar in format to the ECERS, the *Family Day Care Rating Scale* (FDCRS) (Harms & Clifford, 1989), and the *Infant/Toddler Environment Rating Scale* (ITERS) (Harms, Cryer, & Clifford, 1990), but the content is specific to the school-age care group.

The SACERS is composed of 43 items grouped under 6 subscales: Space and Furnishings, Health and Safety, Activities, Interactions, Program Structure, and Staff Development. There is also a set of 6 supplementary items for centers that include children with special needs. As in the other scales, each item is arranged as a 7-point scale with descriptors for each of the odd numbers: (1) inadequate, (3) minimal, (5) good, (7) excellent. An *inadequate* (1) rating represents a lack of care that compromises children's development, a *minimal* (3) rating is indicative of a custodial level of care, whereas a *good* (5) rating describes the basic dimensions of developmentally appropriate care, and an *excellent* (7) rating describes high quality care that expands children's experiences, extends their learning, and provides warm and caring support. The SACERS is meant to be used in center-based care, not in family child care homes.

Although the SACERS follows the format of the ECERS, FDCRS, and ITERS, readers familiar with those scales will notice two additions. First, a Training Guide has been included in the SACERS manual. It contains activities to prepare observers to be accurate users of the scale. Second, the SACERS contains sample questions to make it easier to ask for information that the observer is not able to see. These questions are included in the Notes for Clarification and indicate the level of quality they address. For example, Q(5) means that the information is needed to decide on whether to give a score of 5.

The SACERS was designed to be comprehensive yet easy to use, so that it would be helpful for classroom staff as a self-evaluation, for agency staff in supervision and monitoring, and for researchers who may wish to include a measure of global quality in their school-age child care projects. The SACERS can also be used in teacher training and as a guide for developing new programs.

RELIABILITY AND VALIDITY

Reliability of the SACERS subscales and total scores was assessed in three ways: internal consistency was calculated using Cronbach's Alphas; inter-rater reliability was measured using the Kappa statistic which corrects for chance agreements; and inter-rater reliability was estimated using intraclass correlations. Validity was assessed in two ways: content validity was assessed using expert ratings of each item's importance to their definition of quality; and construct validity was assessed by correlating SACERS total and subscale scores with staff training and staff-to-child ratios.

Data from 24 after-school programs in two Canadian provinces, Quebec and Ontario, were used to calculate Cronbach's Alphas, Kappas, and construct validity. Two observers independently rated each class on the SACERS during a single visit. One observer rated all 24 classrooms. The second observer was one of five other trained raters. Intraclass correlations require that the same two independent observers rate all groups: these data were available for 13 of the 24 settings. No reliability data was available on the Special Needs Supplementary Items as none of the centers included exceptional children. However, content validity was assessed for the Supplementary Items using expert ratings.

Internal Consistency. Cronbach's Alphas for each of the subscales and total scores based on a sample of 24 centers are: Space and Furnishings, alpha=.76; Health and Safety, alpha=.82, Activities, alpha=.86; Interactions, alpha=.94; Program Structure, alpha=.67; Staff Development, alpha=.73; Total Score, alpha=.95. All of these alphas indicate good to excellent internal consistency except Program Structure, which is adequate.

Inter-rater Agreement. Weighted Kappas were calculated for 24 centers, rated independently by two observers. Weighted Kappas for each of the subscales and total score are: Space and Furnishings, .79; Health and Safety, .83; Activities, .86; Interactions, .82; Program Structure, .82; Staff Development, .91; Total Score, .83. All of the Kappas indicate good to excellent inter-rater reliability.

Intraclass Correlations. Intraclass correlations reflect both the relationship of observers' ratings and the size of the differences between observers' ratings. Intraclass correlations were calculated on 13 centers that were observed by the same two independent observers. Correlations for each of the subscales are: Space and Furnishings, r=.87; Health and Safety, r=.95; Activities, r=.92; Interactions, r=.93; Program Structure, r=.99; Staff Development, r=.99; Total Score, r=.96. All of the intraclass correlations reflect excellent reliability.

Content Validity. Content validity was assessed by asking nine recognized experts from the United States and Canada to rate the importance of each SACERS item to their intuitive definition of high quality on a 5-point scale (1=not important to 5=very important). A mean rating of 4.5 to 5 was found for 91% of the items. The overall mean rating of the items was 4.8. The lowest mean rating assigned to any item was 3.9. The scale can thus be described as having excellent content validity.

Construct Validity. SACERS total and subscale scores were correlated with staff training and staff-to-child ratio. Staff training was estimated by assigning a score between 0 and 5 to indicate the highest level of education attained. For example, a score of 5 was assigned if the staff member had completed a college degree in early childhood education or a related field; a score of 4 was given for completion of a college degree in a field unrelated to early childhood education; a score of 3 if the staff member was currently enrolled in an early childhood education or child development program; a score of 2 if the staff member was currently enrolled in a program unrelated to early childhood; a score of 1 for a high school diploma; and a score of 0 if the staff member had not completed high school. Staff-to-child ratios were determined by dividing the total number of children enrolled in the group by the number of staff members assigned to supervise the group.

Staff training has moderate positive correlations with Space and Furnishings (r=.31), Interactions (r=.29), Program Structure (r=.40), and Total Score (r=.29). Staff-to-child ratios have moderate negative correlations with Health and Safety (r=-.40), Activities (r=-.39), Staff Development (r=-.24), and Total Scores (r=-.30). While these correlations are only moderate, they are based on a relatively small sample of 24 groups. They represent good construct validity within the constraints imposed by sample size, although more research is needed to confirm construct validity.

SUMMARY

These results support the use of SACERS total and subscale scores to describe overall quality and quality in specific areas, respectively. A short form of the SACERS using 17 of the items on the scale has been developed for research use by White, Marchessault, Li, and Bouchard (1994). A description of the items and the psychometric properties of the short form may be obtained from the authors.

Prior to publication, minor revisions were made to the SACERS items based on the reliability and validity results and on feedback from observers and expert reviewers.

REFERENCES

Abbott-Shim, M., & Sibley, A. (1987). *Assessment profile for early childhood programs: Manual administration.* Atlanta, GA: Quality Assist.

Albrecht, K. (1991). *Quality criteria for school-age child care programs.* Alexandria, VA: Project Home Safe.

Baillargeon, M., Betsalel-Presser, R., Joncas, M., & Larouche, H. (1993). One child, many environments: Continuity or discontinuity in kindergarten and school-based day care programs? *Alberta Journal of Education Research, 39,* 127-142.

Betsalel-Presser, R., & Joncas, M. (1994). Le partenariat: Un défi pour l'enseignante du préscolaire et de l'éducatrice du service de garde en milieu scolaire. *Actes du 66ème Congrès de l'Association Générale des Instructrices et Instructeurs des Ecoles et Classes Maternelles Publiques* (AGIEM), Nantes, France.

Galambos, N., & Garbarino, J. (1983). Identifying the missing links in the study of latchkey children. *Children Today, 13,* 2-4.

Harms, T., & Clifford, R. M. (1980). *Early childhood environment rating scale.* New York: Teachers College Press.

Harms, T., & Clifford, R. M. (1989). *Family day care rating scale.* New York: Teachers College Press.

Harms, T., Cryer, D., & Clifford, R. M. (1990). *Infant/toddler environment rating scale.* New York: Teachers College Press.

Jacobs, E. V., White, D. R., Baillargeon, M., & Betsalel-Presser, R. (1991). School-age child care: A preliminary report. *Proceedings of the Child Care Policy and Research Symposium. Occasional Paper #2.* Toronto: Child Care Resource and Research Unit.

Lero, D. S., Goelman, H., Pence, A. R., Brockman, L. M., & Nuttall, S. (1992). *Parental work patterns and child care needs : The Canadian national child care study.* Ottawa: Statistics Canada.

O'Connor, S. (1991). *Assessing school-age child care quality.* Unpublished manuscript, Wellesley College, School-Age Child Care Project, Wellesley, MA.

Seligson, M., & Allenson, M. (1993). *School-age child care: An action manual for the 90's and beyond.* Wesport, CT: Auburn House.

Seppanen, P., deVries, D. K., & Seligson, M. (1993). *National study of before- and after-school programs.* Washington, DC: U.S. Department of Education, Office of Policy and Planning.

Vandell, D. L., & Corasaniti, M. A. (1988). The relations between third graders' after school care and social, academic, and emotional functioning. *Child Development, 59*(4), 868-875.

Vandell, D. L., Henderson, V. K., & Wilson K. S. (1988). A longitudinal study of children with day care experiences of varying quality. *Child Development, 59*(5), 1286-1292.

White, D. R. (1990). *After-school child care: A service for children?* Paper presented at the Learned Societies, Canadian Society for the Study of Education, Victoria, BC.

White, D. R., Marchessault, K., Li, W., & Bouchard, C. (1994). Reliability and validity studies of the *School-Age Care Environment Rating Scale.* (Technical Report). *CRDH Bulletin.* Montréal: Concordia University.

Instructions for Using the SACERS

It is important to be accurate in using the SACERS, whether you use the scale in your own program for self-assessment, or as an outside observer for program monitoring, program evaluation, or research. It is preferable to participate in a training sequence led by an experienced SACERS trainer following the Training Guide on pages 38-40. However, if such training is not available to you, follow the steps listed below before attempting to rate a program.

1. Read the entire scale carefully, including the Items and the Notes for Clarification with the sample questions. In order to be accurate, all ratings have to be based as exactly as possible on the descriptions provided in the scale items.

2. Ratings are to be assigned in the following way:

- Ratings are based on the current situation that is observed or reported, not on future plans.
- When deciding on the rating for an item, read the descriptions beginning with those under 1.
- A rating of 1 is the maximum score given if any part of that description applies.
- A rating of 2 is given if no part of 1 and half or more of 3 apply.
- A rating of 3 or 5 is given only if all parts of the description are met. Please note that all descriptions in 3 must be met before any higher rating is given for an item.
- A midpoint rating of 4 or 6 is given when all of the lower and half or more of the next higher description apply.

- A rating of 7 is given only when all of the description in 5 plus all of the description in 7 apply.

3. A block of at least 2 hours should be set aside for observation and rating if you are an outside observer, that is, anyone who is not a member of the teaching staff, including program directors, licensing personnel, and researchers.

4. Before you begin your observation, ask the person in charge of the program to give you a brief tour of the facility and an overview of the space used and the organization of the program. If the program is organized into self-contained groups, select one group to observe, and follow it for the observation period. If the program is run as one large group, observe the entire program.

5. During your observation, be careful not to disrupt the ongoing activities:

- Maintain a neutral facial expression.
- Do not interact with the children unless you see something dangerous that must be handled immediately.
- Do not talk to or interrupt the staff.

6. The rating scale should be kept readily available and consulted frequently during the entire observation. Be sure to read the Notes for Clarification when they are provided for an item. All ratings should be circled and comments written on the score sheet while observing. Ratings should not be entrusted to memory for later

recording. The score sheet provides a convenient way of recording the scores for items, subscales, and total, as well as your comments.

- The working copy of the score sheet included as the centerfold of this book may be removed for ease in reading the scale. Additional copies of the score sheet are available from Teachers College Press.

- It is advisable to use pencil on the score sheet during the observation. The final score sheet entries should be written clearly and be dark enough to photocopy, should that be necessary. The scores you finally decide on should be circled.

- The score sheet can be marked to indicate which item(s) you need to ask questions about in order to get additional information. Underline the highest score that can be assigned to the item(s) based on your observation. Then put a question mark near the item(s) that require a question, and indicate the nature of the question by writing key words near the question mark. By preparing your score sheet in this way, you can ask questions systematically in a short period of time. Remember to check the Notes for Clarification to see whether sample questions are included for the item(s).

- The score sheet can also be used to briefly indicate the reasons for each of your scores. Key words describing what was observed can serve to remind you about the reasons for your decisions.

7. There are some quality indicators that will not be observed during your visit. Therefore, it will be necessary to interview the director or a classroom staff member to complete the SACERS.

- Let the staff member know that you will need about half an hour when she or he is free of responsibility for the children to ask questions about things you did not see.
- During your observation, note on your score sheet the items and the descriptors you need to ask questions about.
- Take some time after the observation to review the sample questions in the Notes for Clarification. The questions are only suggestions. You should feel free to alter questions to make them more appropriate.

- You may also have to ask questions about some items for which sample questions have not been provided. You can jot these down on the score sheet.
- Ask questions on one item at a time, and take notes or decide on a score before you move to the next item.
- Ask only those questions needed to decide whether a higher score is possible.

It is important to ask questions in a nonjudgmental manner. We all know that questions can be threatening, so the observer needs to put as little pressure as possible on the person who is answering. It is also important to ask open-ended questions that do not give away the answer you are looking for.

Put yourself in the place of the caregiver who has to answer the following questions. How would you feel about each of these questions?

- "Don't you worry about the fact that none of your staff have first aid certificates?"
- "Because I was not here to see what happens when children come in and leave, could you tell me about how children's arrival and departure is handled?"
- "Describe your cultural awareness curriculum."
- "Are there additional materials to which children have access?"

You can see that questions which imply disapproval (such as #1) put people on the defensive. Questions that include abstract terms (such as #3) are hard to understand. It is better to be more specific in your questioning. For example, you might ask, "How do you handle holidays?" or "Do you have any multi-racial books?" Questions that are prefaced by a short explanation about why you need to ask them (such as #2) seem less threatening. The open-ended question about whether there are additional materials (such as #4) also seems very matter of fact.

Further information and activities for training observers to use the SACERS are included in the Training Guide on pages 38-40.

Items and Subscales of the SACERS

1. * Examples are given only to clarify the indicator by illustrating some of the things that may be seen. The indicator is being rated, not the examples. Different examples may be observed.

2. * The intent of this indicator is that younger children are not in competition with older children for play space. Therefore, if the schedule is organized for separate use of the space by different age groups, give credit for this indicator.

3. * It must be possible to supervise space for privacy where children can play alone or in very small groups.

   Q (7) If a child wants to play alone, is there a place to do so? May the child bring materials into the private space? Are activities set up for individuals or very small groups in areas away from the general activity areas?

Before using the Scale, read the Instructions for Scoring.

	Inadequate		Minimal		Good		Excellent
	1	2	3	4	5	6	7

SPACE AND FURNISHINGS

1. Indoor space

Inadequate (1)
- Insufficient space for number of children.
- Space lacks adequate lighting, ventilation, temperature control, or is excessively noisy.
- Space in poor repair (Ex*: peeling paint on walls and ceiling; rough, damaged floors).

Minimal (3)
- Sufficient indoor space for number of children enrolled.
- Adequate lighting, ventilation, temperature control, and acceptable noise level.
- Space in good repair (Ex: floors free of damage; walls in good condition; no peeling paint).

Good (5)
- Ample indoor space for children (Ex: spacious areas which allow children to move around freely; space for furnishings and activities without limiting children's movement).
- Good ventilation, some natural lighting through windows or skylight.
- Space well maintained (Ex: floors cleaned, carpeting vacuumed, trash cleared).

Excellent (7)
- Space is aesthetically pleasing (Ex: light, open, airy feeling).
- Natural light can be controlled (Ex: adjustable blinds or curtains).
- Ventilation can be controlled (Ex: windows open; ventilating fan used by staff).

2. Space for gross motor activities

Inadequate (1)
- No outdoor or indoor space specifically used for gross motor activities.
- Outdoor space lacks protection from the elements (Ex: lacks shade, windbreak, drainage).

Minimal (3)
- Some space available outdoors or indoors for gross motor play on a daily basis.
- Outdoor space has some protection from the elements.

Good (5)
- Ample space outdoors and some space indoors available daily (Ex: gym, yard).
- Outdoor space has a variety of surfaces suitable for different types of play (Ex: asphalt for basketball; grass or other suitable surface for baseball, soccer).

Excellent (7)
- Ample, pleasant, and varied space both outdoors and indoors available daily.
- Younger children have a separate space from older children.*
- Convenient access to outdoor space.

3. Space for privacy*

Inadequate (1)
- No possibility to be alone or in a small group, protected from intrusion by others.
- Staff discourage children from being alone (Ex: children continuously expected to be part of group activities).

Minimal (3)
- Children are allowed to find space to be alone, providing that it can be supervised (Ex: in play equipment, behind furniture).

Good (5)
- Space set aside for individuals or small groups, protected from intrusion by others (Ex: loft area in room).
- Children are permitted to create their own private spaces (Ex: can move some furnishings to create privacy).
- Spaces are easy to supervise while ensuring privacy.

Excellent (7)
- Children may bring self-selected materials into private spaces.
- Staff set up activities suitable for individual or small group use in private areas, away from general group activities.

Notes for Clarification

4. * An interest center is a place where materials are arranged for use within an appropriately equipped play space. For example, an art interest center would have art materials near easels or tables on which materials can be used.

   † Accessible means children can get the materials easily by themselves.

   ‡ Available means materials are somewhere in the center, but children may not be able to get them by themselves.

   Q (7) Are there additional materials to which children have easy access? Where are they stored?

   ** Rate either Item 4 or Item 4a. Ask whether homework is part of the program in order to decide if 4a is to be rated.

5. * Basic materials: Lunch/snack tables and chairs of appropriate size for each age group; mats or cots; cubbies or other place for storing children's things.

   † Mats or cots for nap time are not required for older children.

   ‡ Furniture should be comfortable and suitable to children's size. For example, children's feet should be able to rest on floor when seated. Table height should allow children's knees to fit under the table and elbows above the table.

6. * Basic materials: Tables and chairs, easel or art table, open shelves for storage of materials.

	Inadequate 1	2	Minimal 3	4	Good 5	6	Excellent 7
4. Room arrangement	• Use of space not defined (Ex: no interest centers* in large room or several small rooms with no definition of specific purposes). • Rooms inconveniently arranged (Ex: traffic patterns interfere with activities). • Supervision is difficult.		• At least one interest center with clearly defined purpose accessible to children.† • Other play spaces are used by children. • Easy visual supervision of centers and other play spaces.		• Three or more interest centers defined and conveniently equipped (Ex: water provided if needed, shelving adequate). • Quiet and noisy centers separated. • Arrangement of centers or rooms to promote independent use by children (Ex: labeled, open shelves). • Furnishings do not overcrowd rooms.		• Centers selected to provide a variety of learning experiences (Ex: area for art or other messy activities, computer corner, table for board games). • Additional materials available‡ to add to or change centers or rooms.
4a. When doing homework is part of the program**	• Everything listed above plus no separate area for homework or other quiet study.		• Everything listed above plus separate area for homework or other quiet study.		• Everything listed above plus separate area that is quiet, not crowded, and has suitable furniture for homework or other quiet study.		• Everything listed above plus easy access to areas where reference materials are stored (Ex: library is open, computer accessible).
5. Furnishings for routine care (eating, nap, storage of children's possessions)*	• Insufficient number of basic furnishings for eating, nap,† storage of children's possessions. • Furnishings are in poor repair.		• Sufficient number of routine-care furnishings. • Furnishings are in good repair.		• Routine-care furnishings are appropriately sized.‡		• Daily upkeep of all routine care furnishings (Ex: table tops washed).
6. Furnishings for learning and recreational activities*	• Insufficient number of basic furnishings for learning and recreation.		• Sufficient number of basic furnishings in good repair for learning and recreational activities. • Sufficient, convenient storage for materials.		• Basic furnishings for learning and recreational activities of appropriate size, accessible for daily use, and well maintained. • Some space for display of work done by children in the school-age care group and materials of interest to the group.		• Full range of learning and recreational activity furnishings used regularly (Ex: sand/water table, woodworking bench, or computer). • Provision for appropriate independent use of materials (Ex: labeling or other guidance).

Notes for Clarification

8. * Examples of stationary equipment: jungle gym, slide, swing set, basketball hoop, T-ball pole, hopscotch square.

    Examples of portable equipment: balls, bats, jump ropes, Nerf balls.

    Q (7) Is the gross motor equipment rearranged from time to time? If so, about how often?

9. * The program host is the agency that provides the space for the school-age child care program. Program hosts include schools, community centers, and preschool child care centers, among others. Shared facilities may include the classrooms, library, gym, swimming pool, computer room, playground, meeting rooms, audio-visual room.

    † Play space that is set aside to be used primarily by the school age care program, where their materials may be left out and their program work is displayed on the bulletin boards, is considered dedicated space even if it is shared by another group when the school age program is not in session.

    Q (3) Does the program have space assigned to it that no one else uses? Is the program allowed to use other facilities in the building, for example, the gym, pool, or computer room?

    Q (5) How often can the program use these facilities? When you use the gym or computer room, are children from outside the program allowed to use them as well?

    Q (7) Which areas can be used on a daily basis?

	Inadequate 1	2	Minimal 3	4	Good 5	6	Excellent 7
7. Furnishings for relaxation and comfort	• No upholstered furniture, cushions, or rugs available for children to use. No provision for "softness" in environment.		• Some "softness" in environment (Ex: rug in play space or some upholstered furniture available to children). • Soft furnishings are clean and in good repair (Ex: no tears in fabric, pillow covers washed regularly).		• Softness regularly accessible to children (Ex: cushions in reading area, couches in music/listening area, several carpeted areas).		• Planned cozy area plus "softness" available in other areas (Ex: living room area to relax in).
8. Furnishings for gross motor activities*	• No stationary gross motor equipment indoors or outdoors. • Stationary equipment in poor repair or not age appropriate. • No portable materials to play individual or group gross motor games. • Portable materials in poor repair (Ex: balls not inflated, racket strings broken).		• Some appropriate stationary gross motor equipment in good repair either indoors or outdoors. • Some portable materials to play individual and group gross motor games.		• Variety of stationary gross motor equipment readily available. • Stationary equipment is sturdy, age appropriate, and stimulates many skills. • Variety of portable materials to play individual and group gross motor games.		• Some equipment is imaginative, flexible, and frequently rearranged by staff and children to maintain interest (Ex: movable pieces may be added to equipment). • Several different pieces of equipment for a variety of skill levels. • Portable materials for individual and group games are accessible to the children for independent use.
9. Access to host* facilities	• School-age child care program has no play space dedicated to its exclusive use† (Ex: the program is housed in rooms used by other groups earlier or later in the day).		• School-age child care program has some dedicated space and some access to shared facilities when these are not in use by others.		• School-age child care has ample dedicated space. • School-age care program can arrange for exclusive use of a number of shared facilities on a regular basis (Ex: weekly access to school computer center or community pool).		• School-age program has daily use of a number of shared facilities.
10. Space to meet personal needs of staff	• No special staff areas separate from children's areas (Ex: no separate restroom, lounge, storage for personal belongings).		• Separate restroom. • Some storage for personal belongings (Ex: shared locker).		• Lounge area available separate from children's area. • Adult furniture in lounge. • Ample storage for staff belongings.		• Lounge has comfortable furniture in good condition. • Individual, convenient storage for personal belongings with security provisions.

11

11. * During the orientation to the center, while looking at the space used by the program, make sure to observe or ask about access to phone, space for office, storage, individual conferences, and group meetings.

12. * Health policy must be written.

† All adults in contact with children must meet this indicator.

Q (3) Is there a written health policy? What does the health policy cover? What health training is given to the staff?

Q (5) Is the written health policy given to the parents? How do you handle giving medication to children?

Q (7) What is done about health questions that the staff cannot handle?

	Inadequate 1	2	Minimal 3	4	Good 5	6	Excellent 7
11. Space to meet professional needs of staff*	• No access to phone. • No file storage or office space available. • No space available for individual conferences or adult group meetings during program hours. • No storage space for teacher materials (Ex: no space to keep materials staff need to prepare activities).		• Convenient access to phone. • Access to some file storage and office space (Ex: some space provided in office shared with host facility). • Some space available by prior arrangement for individual conferences or adult group meetings during program hours. • Some storage space available for staff materials.		• Access to ample office space and file storage. • Space for conferences and adult group meetings is satisfactory (Ex: dual or shared use does not make scheduling difficult; privacy is assured; adult-sized furniture available). • Ample storage space available for staff materials.		• School-age child care program has separate office space for its own use. • Program has individual conference and group meeting space that is conveniently located, comfortable, and separate from space used for children's program.

HEALTH AND SAFETY

	Inadequate 1	2	Minimal 3	4	Good 5	6	Excellent 7
12. Health policy*	• No written policy concerning what to do if a child gets sick. • No written rules concerning exclusion for contagious illnesses. • No health records for children. • Staff† have not had physical exam and TB test within 2 years.		• Written policy for isolating a sick child and notifying parents. • Written rules for managing contagious illnesses. (Ex: policy covers exclusion, readmission, and notification of all parents). • Records of immunization and other health information kept for each child. • Staff have had physical exam and TB test within last 2 years. • Staff are trained to detect signs of illness, child abuse and neglect, and report when necessary.		• Written health policy given to parents. • Medication given only with written permission from parents and exact instructions on original pharmacy container.		• Arrangements made for a medical consultant, such as a doctor or nurse, to handle health questions from staff.

13. *Q (1, 3, 5)* What is done when a child becomes ill while at the center? What is done if staff suspect that a child is abused or neglected? What is done to improve children's knowledge about good health practices?

    Q (7) What happens if the staff are concerned about a child's physical or mental health?

14. * Emergency and safety policy must be written.

    † The intent of this indicator is that the after-school care staff have either their own files or easy and continuous access to the school's files, if the program is located on the school premises.

    ‡ Annual renewal of first aid certificate is required.

    Q (1, 3) Can you tell me about your emergency and safety policy? Is it written? What does it cover? Do staff receive training in safety and emergency procedures? Who takes care of the group if a staff member is called away for an emergency? Where is the emergency information kept for each child? What does the emergency information consist of?

    Q (5, 7) How many of the staff are required to have first aid certificates, including CPR? How often are they required to renew their certificates? Is at least one person who is certified in first aid and CPR present at all times? Is anyone required to conduct regular inspection of the grounds, facilities, and equipment for safety purposes?

	Inadequate 1	2	Minimal 3	4	Good 5	6	Excellent 7
13. Health practices	• No area set aside for sick child. • No staff to monitor sick child. • Parents not contacted when child is ill. • Children permitted to interact with sick child. • No posting of allergies and other health problems for staff information (Ex: medication schedules ignored).		• Area set aside for sick child but may not be a separate room. • Same staff supervise both the sick child and healthy children without proper health precautions (Ex: staff do not wash hands after contact with sick child). • Children's allergies and medication schedules posted for staff use. • Parents contacted when child is sick. • Staff report suspected child abuse/neglect to proper authorities.		• Child is isolated in a separate room at the first sign of illness. • Staff take proper health precautions when supervising sick child. • Children taught about health practices (Ex: good nutrition, encouraged to follow hygienic practices).		• Staff provide feedback to parents about child's physical and mental health (Ex: concerns about hearing or vision, loss of appetite, withdrawal, aggression, depression). • Staff assist parents to meet children's health needs (Ex: by arranging for referrals and health screening).
14. Emergency and safety policy*	• No written emergency procedures (Ex: what to do when a child is injured; evacuation plans). • Staff are not required to have training in safety and emergency procedures.		• Written safety and emergency procedures. • All staff trained in safety and emergency procedures. • Facility has passed official fire safety inspection. • There are always two adults present, thus allowing one to leave in case of an emergency. • Emergency information for each child is accessible† (Ex: written permission for medical care, phone numbers for child's parent, doctor, and dentist).		• At least one person with current‡ first aid certificate, including CPR, present at all times in the facility. • Regular inspections required of grounds, facilities, and equipment to identify and eliminate potential hazards.		• All regular staff have current first aid certificates, including CPR.

15

15. *Q (1,3) Are there specific emergency evacuation procedures? Are the evacuation procedures practiced regularly? How often? Are parents informed about accidents?*

    Q (5) What is done to monitor safety hazards in the environment? What is done to make children aware of safety rules?

    Q (7) How are safety practices communicated to parents?

16. * If the school notifies the staff of the school-age care program when child is absent, then parent is not required to do so.

    Q (1,3) What is the parents' responsibility regarding absence or lateness? What do you do if a child is absent without prior notification? What do you do if a child is often late? Is attendance recorded?

    Q (5,7) Do you have a system so that parents can leave messages if their child is going to be absent? Do you receive these messages? How do staff and parents work together to achieve regular attendance?

17. *Q (1, 3, 5) What is your procedure for departure?*

    Q (7) How are the children prepared for proper departure and travel behavior?

	Inadequate 1	2	Minimal 3	4	Good 5	6	Excellent 7
15. Safety practice	• Safety problems indoors (Ex: medicines and other hazardous substances not locked away, doors without panic bars). • Hazards present in outdoor area (Ex: equipment unsafe, unfenced play area, hard surface under climbing equipment, glass and trash in yard). • No telephone accessible. • Evacuation procedures not practiced regularly. • No first aid kit accessible.		• No safety problems indoors or outdoors. • Phone accessible for emergency use. • Emergency procedures posted. • First aid supplies well stocked and accessible. • Emergency numbers posted near phone. • Evacuation procedures practiced monthly. • Parents informed about accidents.		• Staff make frequent inspections of grounds, facilities, and equipment for potential hazards, and safety hazards are eliminated or dealt with. • Children taught safety rules.		• Environment planned to avoid safety problems (Ex: younger children separated from older children during active play; outdoor play equipment appropriately sized for each age group). • Safety information shared with parents (Ex: safety plans explained; parents asked to monitor children so that dangerous objects are not brought to the program).
16. Attendance	• Parents are not required to notify staff if their child will be late or absent.* • Attendance is not recorded. • Staff do not contact the parents of children absent without prior notice.		• Parents of children attending day care are asked to call the staff if their child will be late or absent.* • Attendance is recorded. • Staff call parents about unnotified absences or persistent tardiness.		• Center has an answering machine, bulletin board, or other communications system so that parents can leave messages concerning their child's upcoming absence. • Staff check messages from parents frequently.		• Staff discuss attendance problems with parents and work together to achieve regular attendance.
17. Departure	• No clearly defined departure procedure. • When calling for their child, parents are not required to come into the facility and indicate that the child is leaving for the day. • No check-out procedures for children who are bussed home or who go home on their own.		• When calling for their child, parents are required to come into the facility and sign the child out. • Parents are required to notify staff of alternate arrangements (Ex: other family member or taxi will call for child). • Children who are bussed or who go home on their own are dismissed by a staff member who records departure.		• Only parents or other persons authorized by parents may call for child. • Without prior authorization, child is not permitted to leave until staff obtain verification from parent. • Children who are bussed are escorted to the bus by staff.		• Staff have discussed with children proper and safe departure and travel behavior (Ex: remain seated on bus, use safety restraints in cars, safe crossing of street when leaving vehicle). • Departure is well managed (Ex: staff are actively involved in departure procedures. Parents assume responsibility for their own children after sign out).

Notes for Clarification

18. * If food is brought from home, the center is not responsible for its nutritional value.

    Q (1, 3) How do you make sure that the meals/snacks are nutritious? Are the meals/snacks planned in accordance with official USDA or Canada Food Guide requirements? Where and how is the food stored? What is done about children's food allergies?

    Q (7) Do staff communicate with parents about their children's eating habits and give information about nutrition?

19. *Q (5) Do staff periodically check that the bathroom is clean and the necessary supplies, such as toilet paper, soap, and paper towels are available?*

    Q (7) Are children reminded not to share combs, food, drink, and other personal items?

20. * Materials: felt pens, crayons and pencils for drawing, tempera and watercolor paints, glue, scissors, clay, play dough, and materials for collage, embroidery, weaving, origami, jewelry making.

Name of Program

Name of Teacher

Most children
attending at
one time

Number of children
present today

Ages of children
enrolled

Name of Rater

Number of staff present

Date

Position of Rater

1. Indoor space

1 2 3 4 5 6 7

2. Space for gross
motor activities

1 2 3 4 5 6 7

3. Space for privacy

1 2 3 4 5 6 7

4. Room arrangement

1 2 3 4 5 6 7

4a. For homework

1 2 3 4 5 6 7

5. Furnishings for
routine care

1 2 3 4 5 6 7

6. Furnishings
for learning/
recreational
activities

1 2 3 4 5 6 7

7. Furnishings for
relaxation and
comfort

1 2 3 4 5 6 7

8. Furnishings for gross
motor activities

1 2 3 4 5 6 7

9. Access to host
facilities

1 2 3 4 5 6 7

10. Space to meet
personal needs of
staff

1 2 3 4 5 6 7

11. Space to meet
professional needs
of staff

1 2 3 4 5 6 7

TOTAL
Space & Furnishings
Items 1–11

12. Health policy

1 2 3 4 5 6 7

SCHOOL-AGE CARE ENVIRONMENT RATING SCALE

Teachers College Press

13. Health practices

1 2 3 4 5 6 7

14. Emergency and
     safety policy

1 2 3 4 5 6 7

15. Safety practice

1 2 3 4 5 6 7

16. Attendance

1 2 3 4 5 6 7

17. Departure

1 2 3 4 5 6 7

18. Meals/snacks

1 2 3 4 5 6 7

19. Personal hygiene

1 2 3 4 5 6 7

TOTAL
Health and Safety
Items 12–19

20. Arts and crafts

1 2 3 4 5 6 7

21. Music and
     movement

1 2 3 4 5 6 7

22. Blocks and
     construction

1 2 3 4 5 6 7

23. Drama/theater

1 2 3 4 5 6 7

24. Language/reading
     activities

1 2 3 4 5 6 7

25. Math/reasoning
    activities

1   2   3   4   5   6   7

26. Science/nature
    activities

1   2   3   4   5   6   7

27. Cultural awareness

1   2   3   4   5   6   7

TOTAL
Activities
Items 20–27

28. Greeting/
    departing

1   2   3   4   5   6   7

29. Staff-child
    interactions

1   2   3   4   5   6   7

30. Staff-child
    communication

1   2   3   4   5   6   7

31. Staff supervision of
    children

1   2   3   4   5   6   7

32. Discipline

1   2   3   4   5   6   7

33. Peer interactions

1   2   3   4   5   6   7

34. Interactions
    between staff and
    parents

1   2   3   4   5   6   7

35. Staff interaction

1   2   3   4   5   6   7

36. Relationship be-
    tween program
    staff and class-
    room teachers

1   2   3   4   5   6   7

TOTAL
Interactions
Items 28–36

Copyright © 1996 T. Harms, E. V. Jacobs, & D. R. White
ISBN 0-8077-3508-6

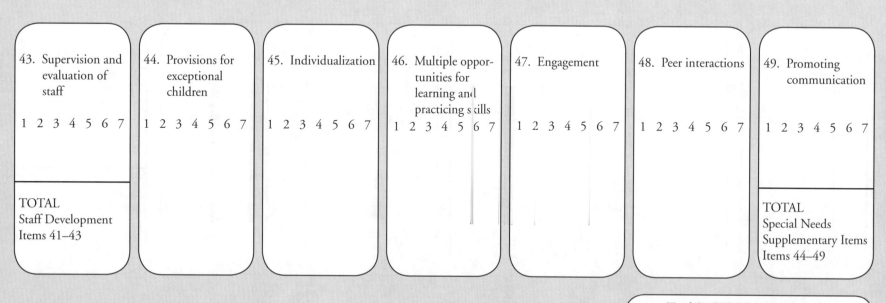

37. Schedule

1 2 3 4 5 6 7

38. Free Choice

1 2 3 4 5 6 7

39. Relationship between program staff and program host

1 2 3 4 5 6 7

40. Use of community resources

1 2 3 4 5 6 7

TOTAL
Program Structure
Items 37–40

41. Opportunities for professional growth

1 2 3 4 5 6 7

42. Staff meetings

1 2 3 4 5 6 7

43. Supervision and evaluation of staff

1 2 3 4 5 6 7

TOTAL
Staff Development
Items 41–43

44. Provisions for exceptional children

1 2 3 4 5 6 7

45. Individualization

1 2 3 4 5 6 7

46. Multiple opportunities for learning and practicing skills

1 2 3 4 5 6 7

47. Engagement

1 2 3 4 5 6 7

48. Peer interactions

1 2 3 4 5 6 7

49. Promoting communication

1 2 3 4 5 6 7

TOTAL
Special Needs
Supplementary Items
Items 44–49

Total SACERS Score_____
(Items 1–43)

SCHOOL-AGE CARE ENVIRONMENT RATING SCALE
Teachers College Press

Copyright © 1996 T. Harms, E. V. Jacobs, & D. R. White
ISBN 0-8077-3508-6

	Inadequate 1	2	Minimal 3	4	Good 5	6	Excellent 7
18. Meals/snacks	• Meals/snacks not appropriately timed for children (Ex: irregularly or rigidly scheduled). • Meals/snacks are of questionable nutritional value* (Ex: do not meet USDA or Canada Food Guide requirements). • No provision for proper food storage. • No provision for sanitary food service (Ex: children eat on floors or on dirty tables).		• Meals/snacks eaten on a regular schedule. • Provision for proper food storage. • Meals and snacks meet USDA or Canada Food Guide requirements. • Children's allergies and other food restrictions considered in food preparation and service. • Food eaten under sanitary conditions. • Menus for meals and snacks posted for parents' information.		• Staff member(s) sits with children and provides pleasant social environment during meals and when possible at snacks. • Small group size at tables permits conversation. • Sufficient amount of food provided for children (Ex: second servings available; if food brought from home is forgotten, supplementary food is available; extra snacks for children who want them at end of day).		• Eating time is planned as a learning experience and discussion time (Ex: including children in preparation, cooking, and serving of food; discussion of children's interests and events of the day; sharing information about nutritional value of foods). • Information shared with parents about nutritional value of foods and children's eating habits.
19. Personal hygiene	• Little attention paid to personal hygiene by staff and children (Ex: hand washing neglected before eating, after toileting or blowing nose). • Tissues, paper towels, soap, and water not accessible. • Bathrooms are not clean.		• Some attention paid to personal hygiene. • Tissues, paper towels, soap, and water are accessible. • Bathrooms are clean (Ex: used tissues and paper towels in trash cans, toilets flushed).		• Hand washing is part of daily routine before eating, after messy activities, outdoor play, and toileting. • Staff periodically check bathroom cleanliness and supplies.		• Personal hygiene is part of educational program to promote good health care habits. • Children have their own toothbrushes and use them after eating. • Children are taught not to share personal items such as combs, or food and drink.

ACTIVITIES

	Inadequate 1	2	Minimal 3	4	Good 5	6	Excellent 7
20. Arts and crafts*	• Art materials not accessible for children to use as a free choice activity. • Regimented use of materials (Ex: mostly teacher-directed projects).		• Some materials accessible for free choice daily. • Materials are in good condition (Ex: felt pens not dried out, clay soft enough to work). • Staff help available when needed.		• Variety of materials accessible for free choice daily. • Individual expression and free choice encouraged. • Very few activities require following an example.		• Opportunity to learn new skills and complete long range projects (Ex: sculpting, pottery, embroidery).
21. Music and movement	• No provisions made for music/movement activities (Ex: no cassette player, tapes, or musical instruments).		• Some provisions for musical experiences weekly (Ex: cassette player or musical instruments).		• Music activities available as a free choice (Ex: listening to tapes or CDs, dancing). • Variety of cassettes, dance props, musical instruments accessible to children.		• Music or movement instruction provided weekly as either individual or group activity (Ex: musical instrument, choral singing, dance).

19

22. * Materials: Blocks of various shapes and sizes, Lego, Lincoln Logs, Meccano; carpentry tools and supplies.

23. * Materials: dress up clothes, costumes, props, puppets.

24. * Materials: Books, dictionaries, encyclopedia, story records, picture lotto, other picture card games, and language games such as Pictionary, crossword puzzles, Junior Scrabble.

    Q (7) Are visits to the library (either in school or to the community library) part of the activities program? How often do the children and staff visit the library? Do children bring books from home to share with the group? Do staff help children write their own stories, poems, and newspapers periodically?

25. * Materials:

    For K—Puzzles, number games, dominoes, Veritec, board games (Ex: Chutes and Ladders).

    For Grades 1 and up—Chess, Checkers, Veritec, board games (Ex: Stratego, Monopoly).

	Inadequate		Minimal		Good		Excellent
	1	2	3	4	5	6	7
22. Blocks and construc- tion*	• No construction materials accessible. • No space set aside for construction activities.		• Some construction materials accessible as a free choice activity weekly. • Appropriate space for use of materials. • Materials in good repair.		• Some construction materials accessible daily. • Sufficient materials for 3 or more children to use at one time.		• Variety of construction materials accessible daily. • Age-appropriate, functional carpentry tools and soft wood available for construction projects.
23. Drama/ theater*	• No materials accessible for pretend play or drama. • No support or encouragement offered by staff.		• Some pretend and drama props accessible. • Some support offered by staff.		• Variety of props which support many roles and situations (work, adventure, fantasy). • Staff extend dramatic play by offering suggestions, finding appropriate space for play to continue.		• Pictures, stories, trips used to enrich dramatic play ideas. • Opportunities for developing drama/theatre productions (Ex: children create costumes, write dialogue, plan productions).
24. Language/ reading activities*	• No materials accessible to enhance the development of language/reading skills.		• Some materials accessible to enhance the development of language/reading skills (Ex: books, story tapes, and language games). • Age-appropriate stories read or told on a weekly basis (Ex: felt board stories, book read in installments).		• Many books and age-appropriate language games accessible to the children on a daily basis (Ex: Junior Scrabble, Pictionary). • Staff are responsive and participate in language games when appropriate (Ex: play rhyming games or language games with children). • Children encouraged to use reading/writing in practical situations (Ex: read instructions for games, write letters to friends).		• Staff take children to library to borrow books on a weekly basis. • Children are encouraged to bring favorite books from home to share with the other children. • Staff help children write their own stories, poems, and newspaper.
25. Math/ reasoning activities*	• No age-appropriate games or activities accessible to encourage math/reasoning.		• Some age-appropriate math/reasoning games and activities accessible on a daily basis. • Staff provide help when asked by children.		• Variety of age-appropriate math/reasoning games and activities accessible for free choice daily. • Staff encourage children to practice math/reasoning skills in daily activities (Ex: set table with correct number of plates, divide snacks, record scores for games).		• Math/reasoning games and activities coded for difficulty and introduced when children are ready. • More experienced children are encouraged to teach others new games.

26. * Equipment and materials: Aquarium, terrarium, measuring tools, magnifying glass, magnets, plants and pets, science books.

27. Q (7) What is done to broaden children's appreciation of other cultures? Do you celebrate any holidays? If so, which ones?

28. * Since greeting and departing are important aspects of a program, the observation should be planned to include both, if possible.

   †Escorting is not a consideration if the school-age care program and school classrooms occupy the same or adjacent space.

   If neither greeting nor departing, or only one can be observed, see sample questions below:

   Q (1, 3, 5) Since I was not here to see arrival (departure), could you tell me what happens? How do staff organize arrival and departure? Are children first grade or younger escorted to the center?

   Q (7) Do staff have the opportunity to talk to parents and others responsible for the children during arrival and departure?

	Inadequate 1	2	Minimal 3	4	Good 5	6	Excellent 7
26. Science/ nature activities*	• No equipment or materials are accessible for science or nature activities. • Science or nature activities are not included in the program.		• Some equipment and materials are accessible for science or nature activities (Ex: table with some natural materials displayed; some animals or plants present in the center).		• Variety of science/nature materials accessible daily. • Children are involved in science and nature activities (Ex: help feed animals or water plants, encouraged to add to science/nature display). • Staff encourage questions about science or natural phenomena, and help children find answers.		• Staff extend children's interest and introduce new concepts (Ex: recycling, conservation of water, endangered species). • Field trips to stimulate interest in science, nature, and environment are part of the program (Ex: planetarium, science museum, botanical gardens).
27. Cultural awareness	• No ethnic, linguistic, gender role, cultural, or racial variety visible in materials (Ex: all print materials are about one culture, all visible pictures are of one race, all materials are in one language in areas where bilingualism is prevalent). • Staff display stereotypic or biased approach to children.		• Some ethnic, linguistic, gender role, cultural, or racial variety visible in materials (Ex: multicultural books, pictures of various countries and races, books in more than one language in bilingual community). • Staff do not display stereotypic or biased approach to children.		• Many multicultural materials visible that reflect the diversity of peoples. • Non-sexist materials visible (Ex: pictures and books depicting males and females in nontraditional roles). • Staff display non-biased approach to activities (Ex: girls encouraged to participate in carpentry; boys encouraged to participate in cooking).		• Staff plan activities to broaden children's cultural awareness (Ex: invite storytellers and musicians from different cultures; holidays are celebrated from many religions and cultures). • Staff encourage acceptance and understanding of differences (Ex: discourage derogatory remarks, help children understand and empathize with hurt feelings due to prejudiced comments).

INTERACTIONS

	Inadequate 1	2	Minimal 3	4	Good 5	6	Excellent 7
28. Greeting/ departing*	• Children (K–Grade 1) not escorted† to the center. • Greeting of children is often neglected. • No plans made to integrate children into ongoing activities when they arrive at the center at the end of their school day (Ex: older children arrive later than K children and disrupt their activity).		• Kindergarten children escorted to the center. • Acknowledgment of children's arrival and departure is inconsistent (Ex: not all arrivals and departures are acknowledged).		• Children (K–Grade 1) escorted to center • Plans made to ensure warm greeting, integration, and organized departure for all children. • Staff members take responsibility for greeting, integration, and departure of children (Ex: conversation on arrival, introduction to program for the day).		• Staff use arrival and/or departure as information-sharing time to relate warmly to parents and others responsible for children.

31.   *Q (7) Does anyone provide instruction in team sports? Are there any other activities where staff are needed to help children develop skills?*

	Inadequate 1	2	Minimal 3	4	Good 5	6	Excellent 7
29. Staff-child interactions	• Staff members are not responsive to or not involved with children (Ex: ignore or reject children). • Interactions are unpleasant (Ex: voices sound strained and irritable).		• Staff respond inconsistently (Ex: sometimes warm, sometimes distant with children). • Staff favor or dislike particular children.		• Staff usually respond to children in a warm, supportive manner (Ex: staff and children seem relaxed, voices cheerful, frequent smiling). • Staff show respect for children (Ex: listen attentively, treat children fairly, do not discriminate).		• Staff support autonomous behavior in children (Ex: staff allow children to take the lead in selecting and initiating activities). • Mutual respect exists among staff and children.
30. Staff-child communication	• Staff-child communication is used primarily to control children's behavior and manage routines. • Children's talk not encouraged.		• Staff initiate brief conversations (Ex: ask questions that can be answered yes/no, limited turn-taking in conversations). • Limited response by staff to child-initiated conversations and questions.		• Staff-child conversations are frequent. • Turn-taking in conversation between staff and child is encouraged (Ex: staff listen as well as talk). • Language is used primarily by staff to exchange information with children and for social interaction. • Children are asked "why, how, what if" questions which require longer, more complex answers.		• Staff make effort to talk with each child (Ex: listen to child's description of school day, including problems and successes). • Staff verbally expand on ideas presented by children (Ex: add information, ask questions to encourage children to explore ideas).
31. Staff supervision of children	• No supervision of children in activity areas during play and routines.		• Some supervision of children in activity areas during play and routines, especially in potentially dangerous areas (Ex: outdoor play, climbing apparatus, carpentry).		• Careful supervision of all children adjusted appropriately for different ages and abilities (Ex: younger children supervised more closely). • Children given help and encouragement when needed (Ex: shown how to use new equipment). • Staff show appreciation of children's efforts and accomplishments.		• Staff talk to children about ideas related to their play and help elaborate and extend the activity. • Staff are available to coach team sports and help with activities requiring adult input.

Notes for Clarification

32. *Q (7) Are parents notified about your discipline policy? How is it done? If you have a child with difficult behavior problems, how do you get help?*

34. * Resources for parents: Parent handbook, newsletters, bulletin board, parent conferences, scheduled parent group meetings, parenting materials.

Q (3, 5) How do you inform parents about your program? What kinds of information do you give them? Are there opportunities for parents to participate in the program? Could you describe some of these parent participation opportunities? Are there individual parent conferences for each child?

Q (7) Do you provide information to parents about such things as health care, sports, or cultural events? Do parents help make decisions about the program? For example, are parents on the board? Does parent feedback have an influence on the program?

	Inadequate 1	2	Minimal 3	4	Good 5	6	Excellent 7
32. Discipline	• Program does not have guidelines for discipline practices. • Expectations for behavior are inappropriate for age and developmental level of children. • Discipline is either too strict or too lax. • Harsh discipline techniques are used (Ex: physical punishment, shouting, withholding food, confining children for long periods).		• Program has policy that harsh discipline is never used. • Expectations for behavior are appropriate for each age group. • Staff never use harsh discipline. • Staff usually maintain enough control to prevent children from hurting one another.		• Staff use non-punitive discipline methods effectively (Ex: giving attention for positive rather than negative behaviors; redirecting child from unacceptable to acceptable activity).		• Parents are notified of program's discipline policy in writing. • Staff seek advice from consultant concerning behavior problems.
33. Peer interactions	• Little or no positive peer interaction (Ex: teasing, bickering, fighting are common). • Little or no staff guidance for positive peer interaction. • Peer interaction not encouraged (Ex: talking with peers discouraged).		• Staff deal with negative peer interactions (Ex: stop teasing, bickering, fighting). • Peer interactions encouraged (Ex: children allowed to move freely so natural groupings and interactions can occur).		• Peer interactions usually positive (Ex: cooperation, sharing; children generally play well together). • Staff model good social skills (Ex: are calm, listen, and empathize). • Staff help children develop appropriate social behavior with peers (Ex: staff help children talk through social conflicts).		• Children demonstrate good social problem-solving skills and positive social behavior (Ex: can negotiate solutions, make compromises, work together toward a common goal, empathize with others' feelings). • Staff serve as sounding board and extend children's problem solving skills.
34. Interactions between staff and parents*	• No sharing of information between parents and staff.		• Parent and staff share minimal information (Ex: information limited to rules, fees, attendance schedule). • Parent conferences occur only upon staff or parent request. • Some attempt to welcome parents into the program.		• Parents made fully aware of program policies and practices (Ex: handbook, information sheets about activities, parent meetings). • Regularly scheduled parent conferences. • Parents welcomed as part of program (Ex: parents share a family custom with child's group).		• Information provided on parenting, health care, sports, and cultural activities for families. • Parents involved in decision making roles (Ex: parent representatives on board, yearly evaluation of program, input from parents sought regarding program content).

35. *Q (3, 5, 7) Is there time for staff to communicate necessary information about children in program? Is there time set aside for planning? How often? Are responsibilities and work shared evenly? Are duties specified for each person? How does the program promote positive interactions among staff members?*

36. *Q (3, 5, 7) Do child care staff communicate with the children's teachers? If so, how?*

37. *Q (3) Do children have gross motor activities scheduled daily?*

    Q (5) Can staff make changes in the schedule on their own?

    Q (7) Are field trips and special activities a part of your program?

	Inadequate 1	2	Minimal 3	4	Good 5	6	Excellent 7
35. Staff interaction	• No communication among staff members of necessary information to meet children's needs (Ex: information regarding early departure of child is not communicated). • Interpersonal relationships interfere with caregiving responsibilities (Ex: staff socialize while looking after children or are curt and angry with one another). • Staff duties not shared fairly (Ex: one staff member handles most duties, while another is relatively uninvolved).		• Some information to meet children's needs is communicated (Ex: staff share health information left by parents). • Interpersonal interaction among staff does not interfere with caregiving responsibilities. • Staff duties are shared fairly.		• Child-related information is communicated daily among staff (Ex: information about routines and play activities). • Time set aside for staff communication. • Staff interactions are positive and add a feeling of warmth and support. • Responsibilities are divided so that activities and problems are handled smoothly.		• Staff working with the same group or in the same room have planning time together at least bi-weekly. • Responsibilities of each staff member are clearly defined (Ex: each carries out specific tasks). • Program promotes positive interaction among staff members (Ex: by organizing social events; by encouraging group attendance at professional meetings).
36. Relationship between program staff and classroom teachers	• No communication between school-age child care staff and children's classroom teachers about children and program.		• Some communication between school-age child care staff and children's classroom teachers concerning problems with children and/or program.		• School-age child care staff and classroom teachers communicate regularly.		• School-age care staff and classroom teachers cooperate to meet children's needs.

PROGRAM STRUCTURE

	Inadequate 1	2	Minimal 3	4	Good 5	6	Excellent 7
37. Schedule	• No basic daily routine that is familiar to children. • Schedule is either too rigid, leaving no time for individual interests, or too chaotic with many disruptions.		• Basic daily routine exists that is familiar to children (Ex: arrival, snack, activities occur in the same sequence most days). • Written schedule is posted in center. • At least one indoor and one outdoor activity period (weather permitting) is scheduled daily. • Some scheduled gross motor activity time indoors or outdoors daily.		• Flexibility is possible within the schedule (Ex: longer outdoor play period in good weather). • Several activities that meet the needs of different age groups are available each day. • A variety of activities go on at the same time, some planned and some spontaneous. • Regularly scheduled gross motor time daily on a year-round basis outdoors, weather permitting, or indoors.		• Smooth transitions between activities (Ex: materials ready for next activities before current activities end). • Field trips and special activities scheduled (Ex: program takes advantage of special community events).

38. * Child is permitted to select materials, companions, and as far as possible manage play independently. Adult interaction is in response to child's needs.

    Q (7) Are new materials made available in response to children's interests?

39. * The intent of this item is that the school-age program is given responsibility for decision making. If the program is operating within a child care center, there may not be a director of the school-age program, but there should be one person who participates in decisions affecting the school-age care program.

    Q (1, 3, 5, 7) How are major administrative decisions about the school-age care program made? Who makes the decisions?

40. * Community resources include parks, playgrounds, pools, libraries, museums.

    Q (1, 3, 5, 7) What facilities in the community do you use? How do you prepare for these trips out of the center?

	Inadequate 1	2	Minimal 3	4	Good 5	6	Excellent 7
38. Free choice *	• No opportunity for free choice in the schedule (Ex: children not allowed to choose materials, activities, or play in self-selected groups).		• Some opportunity for free choice in schedule (Ex: at least two activities to choose from offered at the same time). • Children are free to decide not to participate in any activity (Ex: child may choose to be alone, socialize with a few friends, or rest).		• Most of the time, children may choose from a wide variety of age-appropriate games, materials, and activities. • Children may choose their own companions. • Opportunities exist for individual, small group, and large group activities.		• Children encouraged to develop and extend activities which are of interest to them. • New materials to extend choices are added periodically in response to children's interests.
39. Administrative relationship between program staff and program host.*	• Major administrative decisions made without participation of school-age center staff (Ex: budget, hiring, and program decisions made by school board, principal, or board of directors).		• Director/key staff member of school-age program involved in some administrative decisions concerning program.		• Director/key staff member of school-age program is responsible for administration of program (Ex: budget, curriculum, hiring).		• Director/key staff member of school-age care has regular meetings with host of program to resolve difficulties and make plans (Ex: meetings with principal of school, director of YMCA).
40. Use of community resources*	• Community resources not used.		• Some use made of community resources (Ex: visits to parks and playgrounds). • Parent permission obtained for all trips out of center. • Rules of conduct and safety are explained to children prior to trips.		• Regularly scheduled use of recreational and cultural community resources. • Sufficient number of adults are available for supervision (Ex: parents and volunteers augment center staff on trips). • Special trips are carefully planned to ensure a successful experience (Ex: hours that museum is open are verified, transportation arrangements checked).		• Value of trips enhanced by advanced preparation (Ex: children and staff read and discuss background material to make trip more meaningful). • Children's interests are taken into consideration when trips are planned.

Notes for Clarification

41. *Q (1, 3, 5) What does orientation for new staff members consist of? Is there any in-service training? How often does training occur? What does it consist of?*

    Q (7) Is funding provided to attend conferences or courses?

42. *Q (1, 3, 5, 7) Do you have staff meetings? How often? What is discussed?*

43. *Q (1, 3, 5, 7) How often are staff supervised? How is feedback given to staff about their work? Is there opportunity for self-evaluation? Can staff members request help from supervisors?*

	Inadequate 1	2	Minimal 3	4	Good 5	6	Excellent 7

STAFF DEVELOPMENT

	Inadequate	Minimal	Good	Excellent
41. Opportunities for professional growth	• No orientation or in-service training provided for staff.	• Some orientation for new staff including emergency, safety, and health procedures. • Some in-service training provided.	• Thorough orientation provided for new staff members including interaction with children and parents, discipline methods, appropriate activities. • In-service training provided regularly on site (Ex: guest speakers, films, and videos). • Some professional resource materials available on premises (Ex: books, magazines, or other materials on child development and activities for school-age care).	• Support available for director/program leader or staff members to attend courses, conferences, or workshops (Ex: release time, travel costs, conference fees). • Good professional library containing current materials on a variety of school-age child care subjects available on premises.
42. Staff meetings	• No staff meetings.	• Staff meetings held at least every three months to address administrative concerns.	• Regular monthly staff meetings including staff development activities.	• Staff meetings include planned opportunities for staff to share new professional ideas and materials with one another.
43. Supervision and evaluation of staff	• No supervision provided for staff. • No feedback or evaluation provided about staff performance.	• Some supervision provided for staff (Ex: director observes informally, observation done in case of complaint). • Some feedback about performance provided.	• Annual supervisory observation. • Written evaluation shared with staff.	• Staff participate in self-evaluation. • Staff can request help and guidance from supervisor.

44. * An exceptional child is any child whose physical, mental, or emotional needs are not met by the regular program alone.

    † Modifications:

    • In the physical environment, such as ramps, accessible stalls in restrooms

    • In the program, such as specialized materials, equipment, use of supportive services, individually planned program

    • In the schedule, such as shorter day, alternative activities

45. * Refers to the extent to which staff modify tasks, activities, levels of assistance, and reinforcement according to the needs and abilities of each child.

46. * Refers to the extent to which the staff provide multiple opportunities for children to learn and practice the same skill, and the way in which these opportunities are presented.

	Inadequate 1	2	Minimal 3	4	Good 5	6	Excellent 7

SPECIAL NEEDS SUPPLEMENTARY ITEMS

Items 44-49 are to be used in addition to the whole scale when children with special needs are included in the group.
In order to use these items accurately, information is needed about the special needs of the individual children.

44. Provisions for exceptional children*

Inadequate (1)
- No modifications† made to the physical environment, program, and/or schedule for exceptional children.
- Reluctant to admit children with special needs.
- No attempt to assess child's needs or to find out about available assessments.

Minimal (3)
- Minor modifications made to the physical environment, program, and/or schedule to permit child to attend (Ex: exceptional child allowed to play alone if not able to join group activities).
- Some attempt to find out about child's needs or to find out about available assessments.

Good (5)
- Staff have information from available assessments or request assessment of child's needs.
- Staff use assessment information about needs of exceptional children and make modifications in environment, program, and schedule so that children can participate in many activities.

Excellent (7)
- Consultation with professional special educators regularly available to assist in planning individual programs for exceptional children.
- Center staff follow through with activities and interactions recommended by professional special educators to help children meet identified goals.

45. Individualization*

Inadequate (1)
- Little or no individualization (Ex: same activities, procedures, schedule, environment, and consequences for all children).
- Children often fail tasks or cannot participate in ongoing activities.

Minimal (3)
- Some individualization provided (Ex: separate toileting scheduled for children needing special help).
- Staff make minor modifications so that children can be included in some activities.

Good (5)
- Much individualization provided in play activities and routines.
- Children participate successfully in tasks and activities that appropriately challenge their abilities.
- One-to-one and small group activities provided in addition to regular program for exceptional children.

Excellent (7)
- Objectives for special needs children are incorporated into free play and planned activities.
- Staff use interactions with children, room arrangement, materials, and schedule to meet individual needs (Ex: raised picture labels on toy shelves for visually-impaired child; staff sign so hearing-impaired child can participate fully).
- Independence encouraged through environmental modification, appropriate activities, and teaching strategies.

46. Multiple opportunities for learning and practicing skills*

Inadequate (1)
- Staff do not provide repeated opportunities for learning and practicing skills identified as goals for the child.

Minimal (3)
- Staff provide some opportunities for learning and practicing skills, usually in special activities child does alone.

Good (5)
- Repeated opportunities for learning and practicing skills.
- Some instances of skill practice during naturally occurring routines and events.

Excellent (7)
- Frequent use of naturally occurring routines and events to reinforce learning objectives.

47. * Refers to the extent to which children are actively and appropriately involved with materials, people, or activities.

48. * Refers to the extent to which staff members promote social interaction with peers by providing opportunities for interactions to occur, and by prompting, modeling, and reinforcing peer interactions.

49. * Refers to the extent to which the adult serves as a communication model, responds to children's attempts to communicate, and prompts communication use.

	Inadequate 1	2	Minimal 3	4	Good 5	6	Excellent 7
47. Engagement*	• Little appropriate involvement (Ex: much time spent waiting for other children or staff, in inappropriate behavior or wandering).		• Some appropriate involvement during staff-directed activities (Ex: children pay attention during small group work). • Some appropriate involvement during routines and play times.		• Children are appropriately involved most of the time during staff-directed activities, routines, and play times. • Staff interact with children and provide attractive, developmentally appropriate materials to maintain active involvement (Ex: staff guide wandering child to attractive play area; help non-mobile child change activity when ready).		• Transitions between activities, routine care, and play times are arranged so children maintain involvement (Ex: children continue to play until next activity is ready). • Many alternative activities available for children to use independently or in small groups (Ex: child who loses interest in story is allowed to build with Lego).
48. Peer interactions*	• No attempt made by staff to promote peer interactions. • No peer interaction occurs.		• Occasional efforts to promote peer interactions, mostly in special activities not related to ongoing events (Ex: asking for and passing things done in a special small group, but not during lunch).		• Many efforts to promote peer interactions at planned group times (Ex: child given chance to answer question at story time; to help someone else set the table). • Some peer interaction encouraged during free choice activities.		• Many efforts to promote peer interactions during free choice activities. • Frequent efforts to include child with disabilities in appropriate peer interactions throughout the day.
49. Promoting communication*	• Staff do not encourage children's communication (Ex: do not ask questions, ignore children's attempts to communicate). • Communication to children is primarily directive. • Staff do not provide communication options required by child's disability (Ex: do not face hard-of-hearing child when talking; do not provide communication board or use signing to child who is unable to speak).		• Staff provide some communication opportunities during structured activities, using alternative communication options, when necessary (Ex: communication board used during snack time). • Staff occasionally encourage children's communication outside of structured activities.		• Staff adjust speech to children's level of understanding. • Communication with children includes much social conversation and information sharing. • Staff ask developmentally appropriate questions and attend to children's answers. • Alternative communication options used throughout the day. • Staff involve other children in communication with child with disabilities.		• Staff frequently promote children's communication (Ex: give verbal descriptions of ongoing activities, expand on children's talk, prompt or model communication, and reinforce children's attempts to communicate). • Staff use routines and activities throughout the day to reach appropriate communication goals for the children.

Training Guide for the SACERS

A suitable training sequence can be designed to meet the various needs of SACERS trainees by selecting from the following training activities. Training Activities 1-5 cover the basic information and skills needed for all users of the scale. Training Activities 6-8 are required for outside observers, that is, any observer who is not a member of the teaching staff, including program directors, licensing personnel, and researchers. Training Activity 9 is required for program monitors and researchers who need to be trained to a level of inter-rater reliability required by their programs.

PREPARING TO USE THE SCALE

1. Show slides or a TV tape about school-age programs, in order to assure that the trainees have a common understanding of what is meant by quality school-age care. If this is not possible, describe a few typical settings and key issues, and have the trainees discuss these.

2. Present the 49 Items of the SACERS.
    - Have the trainees look over the list of items on page 5 to see the range of topics covered. Point out that the special needs items are used only when a child with disabilities is included in the group.
    - Select one item that interests the trainees and turn to that item in the scale. Notice how the item is set up as a 7-point scale with descriptions under 1, 3, 5, and 7.

3. Have the trainees work in pairs to do the **Scrambled Item** activity on page 39. Allow time for discussion to deal with the concept of levels of quality in the scale. This activity helps the trainee learn to read carefully. The answer key to the Scrambled Item is on page 40.

4. Review the rules for rating (number 2 in the Instructions for using the SACERS on pages 3-4).

5. Have the trainees work in pairs to rate Item 37, Schedule, after reading the **Sample Situation** on page 39. The Sample Situation describes what might be found during an observation, and the activity gives the trainees practice in coring an item. In order for each trainee pair to have the text of both the Sample Situation and the Item accessible simultaneously, suggest that one turn to the Item and the other to the Sample Situation. After the trainees decide on a score, have them explain their reasoning. The answer key to the Sample Situation is on page 40.

6. Discuss the guidelines for asking questions on page 4, and have the trainees complete the activities on questioning. These activities are needed only for outside observers who will have to interview the director or a classroom staff member to complete the scoring of the SACERS.

    In order to practice questioning, have the trainees work in small groups of two to three people. Designate one person to act as the observer and another as the staff member. Select items from the scale for the trainees to use in making up questions. Tell the trainees to check the Notes for Clarification to see if there is a sample question for the item. Trainees should use that question first to see if they get the information they need. If not, they should make up some probing questions to get the specific information they need. Get feedback from the trainee who acted as the staff member about how the questioning went.

CONDUCTING A PRACTICE OBSERVATION

7. It is necessary for outside observers to complete at least one practice field observation, preferably with a partner or two. The number of practice field observations needed varies with the purpose of the training. Research use of the scale requires high inter-rater reliability and therefore may need several practice observations followed by item-by-item reliability checks.

    The purpose of a practice field observation is to provide an opportunity for the trainees to learn to use the SACERS, not to evaluate the group being observed. Be sure to make that point clear to the centers you contact as practice observation sites.

    - Before sending the teams out, discuss considerate observer behavior.
    - Send observers in teams of two to four (depending on the size of the room), for a period of 2 to 3 hours. They should observe together but score independently. Each one will need a scale and a score sheet. If possible, include a team leader who has had some experience with the scale.
    - Conduct the practice observation following the Instructions for Using the SACERS on pages 3-4.
    - All the observers should be present for the questioning of the staff so that questions will only have to be answered once.

DETERMINING INTER-RATER RELIABILITY

8. After completing the observation and independently circling scores for all items on the score sheet, have the team compare their scores, item by item, using a Summary Score Sheet such as the sample shown on page 40. Most important is the discussion of items with discrepant scores that are more than

(text continues on page 40)

TRAINING ACTIVITIES
Scrambled Item

In the following SACERS Item the descriptions for each level of quality are out of order. Read each of these descriptions carefully and decide which description should be labeled inadequate (1), minimal (3), good (5), and excellent (7).

37. Schedule

(a) _____
- Basic daily routine exists that is familiar to children (Ex: arrival, snack, activities occur in the same sequence most days).
- Written schedule is posted in center.
- At least one indoor and one outdoor activity period (weather permitting) is scheduled daily.
- Some scheduled gross motor activity time indoors or outdoors daily.

(b) _____
- No basic daily routine that is familiar to children.
- Schedule is either too rigid, leaving no time for individual interests, or too chaotic with many disruptions.

(c) _____
- Smooth transitions between activities (Ex: materials ready for next activities before current activities end).
- Field trips and special activities scheduled (Ex: program takes advantage of special community events).

(d) _____
- Flexibility is possible within the schedule (Ex: longer outdoor play period in good weather).
- Several activities that meet the needs of different age groups are available each day.
- A variety of activities go on at the same time, some planned and some spontaneous.
- Regularly scheduled gross motor time daily on a year-round basis outdoors, weather permitting, or indoors.

Sample Situation

After reading the following sample situation, turn to Item 37, Schedule, in the scale to decide on a score.

You are observing in a school-age care program that has 20 children ranging in age from 5 to 10 years. When the children come to the center they hang up their coats and put their knapsacks in their cubbies. The snack is set out for 25 minutes, and they may have snack as they wish. You notice that they are free to move to any one of several activity areas set out for them in their room with age appropriate activities. They may also select other activities from cupboards in the room. There is a schedule posted on the wall that shows that indoor and outdoor play are scheduled daily. At 3:45 you follow the whole group to the gym. Some children complain they want to continue playing in the room. A staff member says that they need some exercise and they can't go outside because of the rain. At 4:20 when the games are whistled to an end some of the children ask to stay a little longer to finish the game. The staff remind the children that a local basketball team uses the gym at 4:30 daily so they must return to the room. The children grumble and shuffle their way back to their room.

How would you score this situation? _____

Why did you give this score? _____

one point apart. Have everyone try to understand why the discrepancies occurred and agree on the most appropriate score, if possible. Through the discussion of discrepancies, the scale items and scoring system are clarified and reliability is improved.

One way to determine inter-rater reliability is to assess whether two or more observers who independently rate the same situation at the same time agree on the scores given to an item. It is necessary to examine the individual items to see if raters agree on the scores. A Summary Score Sheet helps you to calculate the percent agreement. To complete the Summary Score Sheet:

- Record the name of the center, the classroom being observed, the date, and the names of the observers on the top of the summary sheet. List all item numbers on the left hand side of the sheet (see sample).
- Record the ratings given by each observer for each item. It is important that these ratings be independent, that is, they should be recorded on each observer's score sheet before any discussion occurs.
- After all the items have been recorded on the Summary Score Sheet, discuss the reasons for differences in scores, starting with scores that differ by more than 1 point. Scores will differ for a variety of reasons: observers may not all see the same activity, they may interpret scoring criteria differently, or they may not read the criteria thoroughly. Some of the differences are errors and can be corrected in future observations. Others may simply be due to the fact that there is some variability in what is seen and in interpretation of the criteria.
- Calculate the percent agreement for each item by dividing the largest number of raters agreeing on a single score by the total number of raters and multiplying by 100. Note the sample showing the first 4 items. For item 1, all 3 raters agreed on a score of 4. Thus, 3 divided by 3 x 100 = 100%. For item 2, two raters agreed on a rating of 3, while a third gave a rating of 2. Since the rule says to take the largest number of raters agreeing on a single rating, the agreement would be 2/3 x 100 therefore 67%. For item 4, where no raters agreed, the raters need to reach consensus on the best score after discussing the descriptors and notes for clarification. The consensus score then becomes the standard against which the other scores are compared. If a score of 2 becomes the standard, then the item would have a 33% agreement (1/3 x 100=33%).

9. Have the trainees complete the scale in a second classroom with a group of two or three observers, and again conduct an item-by-item reliability check in order to reach the level of inter-rater reliability required. Following training, observers typically gain in ease and accuracy with repeated use of the scale. When several observers who have been trained to criterion use the scale in research over a period of time, periodic inter-rater reliability checks are recommended.

Sample Summary Score Sheet

Item	Observer Name			Percent Agreement
	Harms	Jacobs	White	
1	4	4	4	100%
2	3	3	2	67%
3	5	6	6	67%
4	3	2	4	33%

ANSWER KEY
Scrambled Item: 37. Schedule

(a) 3   (b) 1   (c) 7   (d) 5

The inadequate level 1 (b) indicates a lack of schedule or a schedule that is too rigid. For a minimal 3 (a) there has to be a basic routine familiar to the children, and a written schedule with at least one indoor and one outdoor activity period and some scheduled gross motor activity daily. For a 5 (d) flexibility in scheduling is required, with activities going on at the same time for different age groups. In addition to a good activity program, as described in 5, for a 7 (c) there are smooth transitions between activities, and special activities are provided, such as field trips.

Sample Situation: Score 4

This child care program has a basic daily routine, and the schedule is not too rigid, so this should not be rated as inadequate (1). Given that the children seemed to know what to do when they arrived in the center, it appears that the routine was familiar to them. The schedule listed both outdoor and indoor play, with a gross motor activity time scheduled daily. Therefore, this item merits at least a minimal score (3), and we go on to look at good (5). There are a variety of activities going on at the same time, and from the schedule you see that gross motor time is scheduled daily indoors and outdoors. However the staff could not be flexible about indoor gross motor time beyond 4:15, and the schedule was not varied for the children who wanted to continue to play in the room. Therefore, not all of the description for a (5) applies to this center. However, it meets all of the criteria for (3) and half or more of the indicators for (5), so it is given a score of (4).